# Spotlight on™ Social Skills, Interpersonal Negotiation

## by Carolyn LoGiudice & Paul F. Johnson

| Skills | Ages |
|---|---|
| ■ identifying and stating problems clearly | ■ 11 and up |
| ■ understanding others' perspectives and needs | **Grades** |
| ■ determining mutual solutions | ■ 6 and up |

### Evidence-Based Practice

■ Children with limited language skills experience a poor quality of social interactions (Hadley & Rice, 1991; Fujiki et al., 1997; Craig, 1993; Cohen et al., 1998). Such children have greater deficits in social cognitive processing than children with typically developing language. They have particular deficits in identifying the feelings of each participant in a conflict, identifying and evaluating strategies to overcome obstacles and knowing when a conflict is resolved (Cohen et al., 1998).

■ Social skills intervention can improve children's social cognitive skills (Timler et al., 2005).

■ Targeted language intervention with at-risk students may result in more cautionary, socially acceptable behaviors (Moore-Brown et al., 2002). Intervention for adolescents with language impairments may include objectives aimed at improving deficient social communication skills (Henry et al., 1995; Bliss, 1992).

■ Interpersonal Negotiation Skills (INS) are important for social problem resolving (Leadbeater et al., 1989; Selman & Demorest, 1984).

■ Students with language disorders often perform much like younger, typically developing students on measures of pragmatic development (Lapadat, 1991).

■ Only 7% of the information we communicate to others depends upon the words we say; 93% depends on nonverbal communication (Mehrabian, 1971).

■ In selecting remediation targets within social communication among adolescents, clinicians should consider the relative importance of various communication skills in terms of enhancing peer communication. Communication skills involving social perspective taking (including nonverbal language) that focus on another person are more valued by adolescents than skills that focus on the speaker's thoughts or linguistics (Henry et al., 1995).

*Spotlight on Social Skills, Adolescent Interpersonal Negotiation* incorporates these principles and is also based on expert professional practice.

## LinguiSystems

LinguiSystems, Inc.
3100 4th Avenue
East Moline, IL 61244
Phone: 800-776-4332

FAX: 800-577-4555
Email: service@linguisystems.com
Web: linguisystems.com

ISBN 978-0-7606-0778-7

# About the Authors

**Carolyn LoGiudice**, M.S., CCC-SLP, and **Paul F. Johnson**, B.A., are editors and writers for LinguiSystems.  They have collaborated to develop several publications, including *Story Comprehension To Go*, *No-Glamour Sequencing Cards* and *Spotlight on Reading & Listening Comprehension*.  Carolyn and Paul share a special interest in boosting students' language, critical thinking, and academic skills.

In their spare time, Carolyn and Paul enjoy their families, music, gourmet cooking, and reading. Carolyn is learning to craft greeting cards and spoil grandchildren.  Paul, a proud father of three children, also enjoys bicycling, playing music and spending rare moments alone with his wife, Kenya.

# Table of Contents

Introduction ............................................................................ 4

Pretest/Posttest ...................................................................... 6

What Is Interpersonal Negotiation? ....................................... 7

Vocabulary ............................................................................. 8

Making Inferences ................................................................. 11

Multiple Interpretations........................................................ 13

Paraphrasing ......................................................................... 15

Alike and Different................................................................. 17

Explaining Your Thoughts .................................................... 18

Point of View......................................................................... 19

Empathizing .......................................................................... 21

Stating a Problem ................................................................. 24

Talking It Over....................................................................... 27

Stating Solutions................................................................... 28

One-Sided vs. Mutual Solutions ......................................... 30

Reaching a Compromise...................................................... 32

Giving Reasons for Solutions.............................................. 34

Maintaining a Friendship ..................................................... 35

"Fair" Isn't Always Equal ..................................................... 36

Role-Playing Situations ........................................................ 37

Answer Key ........................................................................... 40

# Introduction

Adolescents who have not acquired appropriate social skills on their own are unlikely to develop those skills without specific instruction. Activities in *Spotlight on Social Skills, Adolescent* include explicit teaching, modeling, observation, discussion, role-playing, and other guided practice to spotlight specific social skill areas from different perspectives and with varying everyday situations. These activities can be presented to individual students or small groups of students with similar skill deficits.

Before beginning any social skill training, you should evaluate each student's current performance. Determine whether the student has a performance deficit (has the skills but doesn't use them) or an acquisition deficit (lacks the skills or the discrimination of which behaviors to use in specific situations). The activities in this series are designed for students who need direct instruction and guided practice to acquire and master specific skills. Use the Pretest/Posttest, observation, teacher reports, and/or personal interview to select appropriate lessons to present. These are the books in *Spotlight on Social Skills, Adolescent:*

- Nonverbal Language
- Making Social Inferences
- Emotions
- Conversations
- Getting Along
- Interpersonal Negotiation

Since peer relationships are the most important to the majority of adolescents, this training resource contains content mostly targeted to adolescent concerns and peer relationships. Each activity sheet affords a chance to highlight a specific skill and to facilitate discussing that skill with your students. The more you personalize the activities with examples from the students' particular situations, the more effective your training will be.

*Spotlight on Social Skills, Adolescent: Interpersonal Negotiation* teaches your students to manage everyday conflicts successfully. Negotiation skills emerge and develop through adolescence and are usually first successful in peer relationships. The same skills later generalize to interpersonal negotiation with adults, coworkers and others. These skills are required in order to manage interpersonal negotiation as well:

- Identify and state the problem from each party's perspective or a mutual perspective

- Discuss the problem with the other party; explain personal perspective and listen well to the other party's expressed and implied preferences

- Mutually determine appropriate solutions to satisfy both parties

- Accept compromises and negative outcomes graciously; be a good sport

Research suggests developmental levels of interpersonal negotiation.* Young children don't negotiate; they use physical or verbal action to get what they want or they avoid a conflict

*Selman, R.L. & Schultz, L.H. (1989). Children's strategies for interpersonal negotiation with peers: An interpretive/empirical approach to the study of social development. In T.J. Berndt, & G.W. Ladd, eds., *Peer relationships in child development.* New York: John Wiley & Sons.

altogether.  Next they choose one-sided, all-or-nothing, win/lose solutions to conflicts; they control the other person or submit to what the other person wants.  At a cooperative level, students consciously seek solutions by making requests, giving suggestions, bribing, compromising, or accommodating another person's wishes.  During adolescence, interpersonal negotiation skills are refined via experience and maturation.  Students learn to discuss a conflict situation with the other party, working together to seek mutual goals.  The primary goal at this level is to maintain a solid, long-term relationship with a friend vs. to settle a disagreement just for the immediate moment.

Here are some guidelines to keep in mind as you present the activities in this book to your students.

- Taking another person's perspective is a prerequisite skill for mutual problem solving. Students with weak skills in taking someone else's point of view may benefit from direct training in making general inferences as well as making multiple interpretations about situations.  Such training should emphasize that people can and do feel differently about similar situations due to their life experiences, preferences, etc.  As part of the training, teach your students to ask appropriate questions to learn what someone else thinks or wants.

- Some adolescents cling to the less mature notion that fairness means "everyone gets the same" vs. the more mature concept:  "Fairness means that everyone gets what he or she needs."*  As your students seek options to solve problems, especially in situations involving unequal strengths or circumstances, encourage them to think about what would be fair, which is not necessarily equal.

- Many students with language or social disorders lack confidence in expressing their opinions and suggestions to others.  Teach your students the importance of expressing their own perspectives clearly to avoid being ignored or overpowered in interpersonal negotiations.  Help them role-play interpersonal negotiations to build their confidence, especially for current personal situations they are trying to resolve.

- Some problem solutions would work well for the immediate problem, but would not help to maintain a friendship or long-term relationship.  Talk with your students about the value of prioritizing long-term relationships above immediate peace or satisfaction.

- For more in-depth background and teaching activities, see *Room 28: A Social Language Program* (LinguiSystems, 2004).

We hope you and your students enjoy *Spotlight on Social Skills, Adolescent: Interpersonal Negotiation!*

Carolyn and Paul

*"Fair" Isn't Always Equal.  http://www.ricklavoie.com/fairnessart.html.

5

# Pretest/Posttest

Answer these questions to show what you know about negotiating with someone to settle an issue.

1. Give a good example of a problem between two people that could be solved by negotiation between the people.

   _____

2. What is a mutual solution?

   _____

Paraphrase each comment below.

3. I'd rather do something more active and exciting than just watch TV.

   _____

4. We don't have to decide everything right now.

   _____

Nora and Alana came to a party together. Nora needs to get up early tomorrow morning and she'd like to go home. Alana is having a great time and can sleep in tomorrow.

5. What is Nora's problem? _____

   _____

6. What is Alana's problem? _____

   _____

7. What would be a good way to solve this problem? _____

   _____

Jason and Alex both want to play a computer game designed for one person to play. Tell three different statements they could make to each other to negotiate well.

8. _____

9. _____

10. _____

# What Is Interpersonal Negotiation?

Interpersonal negotiation means that people talk about a problem. They try to think of a compromise that satisfies everyone.

Negotiation works well when people want something they can't divide, like a movie ticket. It also works well when friends have different ideas about what to do together.

Negotiation doesn't work well when someone has more power or authority than you. It also doesn't work when someone threatens you.

Check the box beside each problem that might be solved easily if the people negotiated with each other.

☐ 1. Paula and Rhonda are planning a party. Paula wants to invite 24 friends but Rhonda wants to invite just 4 friends.

☐ 2. Dan was caught cheating on a test and was sent to the office to talk with the principal.

☐ 3. Chloe and Dillon are studying in the same room. Chloe likes to listen to loud music while she works. Dillon prefers total silence while he works.

☐ 4. Darcy and Erick are doing a science project together. Darcy wants to meet briefly every day to work on the project. Erick wants to meet just once to do the whole project.

☐ 5. Trey wants to get an after-school job to earn money, but his mom says he is too young and needs to concentrate on his homework more.

☐ 6. The football coach says everyone on the team must have a *B* average. Ian doesn't think grades should matter to the coach.

☐ 7. Chris and Omar are going to a restaurant for a date. Chris wants to go to her favorite Italian restaurant but Omar wants to try a new Mexican restaurant.

☐ 8. Brad's doctor told him to wear a medical alert bracelet because he has diabetes. Brad doesn't want to wear the bracelet because he doesn't want his friends to know he has diabetes.

☐ 9. Sheila and Mike each want to be the first performer in the school talent show.

☐ 10. Carla and Nikki are shopping in a mall. Carla wants to look for shoes. Nikki wants to buy earrings.

# Vocabulary

Understand and use these words to talk about settling disagreements.

| | |
|---|---|
| alternative | a choice to solve a problem; an option |
| benefit | something good or helpful; an advantage |
| compromise | an alternative to solve a problem in a way that each person gets and loses something |
| conflict | a disagreement between two or more people who have different opinions about the same issue; a challenge to solve; an issue |
| consequence | the result of an action |
| dominate | to control or overpower someone |
| drawback | a disadvantage to an alternative to solve a problem |
| empathy | understanding of how someone else feels in a situation |
| flexible | willing to change your opinion or preferences |
| ineffective | useless |
| inference | a conclusion based on what you see or hear; a good guess |
| interpersonal | involving relations between two or more people |
| long-term | lasting over a long period of time |
| motivate | to give someone a reason to do something |
| mutual solution | a problem solution that considers both people's perspectives |
| mutual | shared equally |
| negotiation | a discussion to reach an agreement or settle a conflict |
| one-sided solution | a problem solution that only considers one person's perspective |
| paraphrase | to restate a message in different words |
| personal | private; having to do with just one person |
| perspective | a person's point of view |
| short-term | lasting only a short period of time; immediate |
| solution | the answer to a problem; something that will solve a problem |
| strategy | a plan to do something in a certain way |
| yield | to give in to someone else's preferences |

# Vocabulary ❷

Choose the best word from the box to complete each sentence.

1. There are at least three _____ we can consider.

2. What would _____ you to clean up your room?

3. A _____ friendship is more valuable than a brief friendship.

4. My friend and I have a _____ about how to keep score during the game.

5. If my _____ is correct, Jody needs some help to take her mind off her problems.

6. It's hard to have _____ with someone in a situation you have never experienced yourself.

7. Your _____ skills are the ways you get along with other people.

8. Let me _____ what you said to make sure I understand.

| |
|---|
| alternatives |
| conflict |
| drawback |
| empathy |
| inference |
| interpersonal |
| long-term |
| motivate |
| mutual |
| paraphrase |
| perspective |
| yield |

9. From my _____, studying with a buddy is more fun than studying by myself.

10. I would rather _____ to someone who really cares about something than fight or argue with the person.

11. Getting grounded for a month would be a real _____ of that solution.

12. Playing soccer well is the _____ goal of everyone on the team.

# Vocabulary

Choose the best word from the box to complete each sentence.

1. What will the _____ be if you don't get the work done on time?

2. During a _____, both people explain their opinions and listen to each other's suggestions about ways to settle a disagreement.

3. My _____ opinion is that students shouldn't have any homework on weekends.

4. If you _____ someone, you are not being a friend to that person.

5. My _____ goal is to avoid an argument right now.

6. What would be a good _____ for our problem?

7. One _____ of a mutual solution is that everyone is satisfied.

8. Our first meeting was _____ in settling our argument, so we set a time for a second meeting.

9. A _____ solution is the opposite of a mutual solution.

10. Neither of us was thrilled about the _____, but at least it settled our disagreement.

11. I can't change the date of my party, but I can be _____ about what time it starts.

12. Listening carefully to the other person is a good _____ when you are trying to settle a disagreement between that person and you.

| |
|---|
| benefit |
| compromise |
| consequence |
| dominate |
| flexible |
| ineffective |
| negotiation |
| one-sided |
| personal |
| short-term |
| solution |
| strategy |

# Making Inferences ❶

We make quick inferences about people, even from a picture. For example, we infer how old someone is, how the person feels and what the person is doing and why. These inferences help us understand how to get along with other people.

Check the box beside each logical inference about the person in this photo.

- ☐  1.  The person is a female.
- ☐  2.  It is a windy day.
- ☐  3.  She likes this dog.
- ☐  4.  The dog likes her.
- ☐  5.  She likes cats.
- ☐  6.  She is a student in middle school or high school.

Answer the questions to make inferences about this picture.

7.  Is the person a male or a female? _____

8.  How old is the person? _____

9.  What is the person sitting in? _____

10. What is the person holding? _____

11. How does the person feel? _____

12. Why does the person feel that way?

_____

_____

# Making Inferences ❷

Make at least two inferences about each picture

1.

- _____
- _____

2.

- _____
- _____

3.

- _____
- _____

# Multiple Interpretations

We can often interpret what we see in more than one logical way.  For example, we could make at least three interpretations in this picture:

- She is covering her mouth because she just made a mistake.

- She is about to burp.

- She is surprised by what she sees.

- She doesn't want to say anything about what she sees.

Make at least two interpretations about what is going on in these pictures.  Then compare your interpretations with two or more people.

- _____

  _____

- _____

  _____

- _____

  _____

- _____

  _____

# Multiple Interpretations ❷

Make at least two interpretations about what is going on in these pictures.  Then compare your interpretations with two or more people.

- _____
  _____

- _____
  _____

- _____
  _____

- _____
  _____

- _____
  _____

- _____
  _____

# Paraphrasing

You can paraphrase what someone says to show you understood what the person meant. To paraphrase, you use different words to say the same message.  Here is an example:

Statement      It drives me crazy when my little brother tags along.

Paraphrase      It bugs you that your brother follows you.

Imagine that a friend said each sentence.  Write a comment to paraphrase each one.

1. I feel bad that I never get to school on time.

 

2. I'd like to know if Olivia is dating anyone.

 

3. I like action movies much more than comedies.

 

4. I really pitched badly for the whole game.

 

5. I can't concentrate with all that noise going on.

 

6. Sonia doesn't pay any attention to me.

 

7. Playing the guitar is more important to me than playing basketball.

 

8. It's hard to know what Byron is thinking because he's so quiet.

 

9. Why doesn't anyone ask me for advice?

 

# Paraphrasing ❷

Imagine that a friend said each comment. Write a comment to paraphrase each one.

1. I'm really struggling with geometry.

   _____

2. I don't think Allison even knows I'm alive.

   _____

3. I'd love to have a whole week without any homework.

   _____

4. If we get there early, the line won't be very long.

   _____

5. It's not safe to walk in that park after dark.

   _____

6. It would be great if Tory would invite me.

   _____

7. I didn't mean to break his glasses.

   _____

8. If we take off right now, no one will even notice.

   _____

9. You're asking for trouble if you bother me.

   _____

10. Tracy was supposed to get here 30 minutes ago.

   _____

11. It bothers me when people talk about me.

   _____

# Alike and Different

People have different opinions about what they like to do. Check the box on the left of each activity you enjoy doing yourself. Then check the boxes on the right to rate how many people your age might enjoy each activity you checked – **all** of them, **most** of them, **some** of them, or **none** of them. Next compare your results with at least three other students in your grade. Talk about how your results are alike and different.

|  |  | all | most | some | none |
|---|---|---|---|---|---|
| ☐ | Reading fiction | ☐ | ☐ | ☐ | ☐ |
| ☐ | Reading nonfiction | ☐ | ☐ | ☐ | ☐ |
| ☐ | Riding a bike | ☐ | ☐ | ☐ | ☐ |
| ☐ | Swimming for fun | ☐ | ☐ | ☐ | ☐ |
| ☐ | Swimming in races | ☐ | ☐ | ☐ | ☐ |
| ☐ | Playing sports | ☐ | ☐ | ☐ | ☐ |
| ☐ | Watching sports | ☐ | ☐ | ☐ | ☐ |
| ☐ | Drawing or painting | ☐ | ☐ | ☐ | ☐ |
| ☐ | Hanging with friends | ☐ | ☐ | ☐ | ☐ |
| ☐ | Going to big parties | ☐ | ☐ | ☐ | ☐ |
| ☐ | Going to small parties | ☐ | ☐ | ☐ | ☐ |
| ☐ | Playing computer games | ☐ | ☐ | ☐ | ☐ |
| ☐ | Playing a musical instrument | ☐ | ☐ | ☐ | ☐ |
| ☐ | Singing | ☐ | ☐ | ☐ | ☐ |
| ☐ | Watching movies alone | ☐ | ☐ | ☐ | ☐ |
| ☐ | Watching movies with someone | ☐ | ☐ | ☐ | ☐ |
| ☐ | Text messaging | ☐ | ☐ | ☐ | ☐ |
| ☐ | Babysitting | ☐ | ☐ | ☐ | ☐ |
| ☐ | Eating popcorn | ☐ | ☐ | ☐ | ☐ |

# Explaining Your Thoughts

To help someone understand what you think, you need to share your thoughts. Practice expressing your thoughts in words. Write a clear statement about how you feel about each issue below. Then speak your thoughts out loud with a partner.

1. sharing a room with someone

   _____

2. getting good grades

   _____

3. being graded for physical education

   _____

4. having a set bedtime

   _____

5. painting/spraying graffiti on public property

   _____

6. having a substitute teacher

   _____

7. graduating from high school

   _____

8. keeping a friend's secret

   _____

9. cheating in school

   _____

10. supporting our military troops

   _____

# Point of View

Two friends can feel differently about the same situation. Read each situation below. Then write what each character probably thinks about the situation.

1. Hao and Lian are studying together for a science test. Hao enjoys science and thinks the test will be easy. He is talking quickly. Lian has trouble understanding what Hao is saying because she doesn't know the material as well as he does.

   What does Hao think? _____

   _____

   _____

What does Lian think? _____

_____

2. Kye and Victor want to go to a water park on Saturday. Kye wants to sleep until 11:00 and then go to the park. Victor needs be home by 2:00 to help his dad with a project. These boys need to plan what time to go to the park and how long to stay there.

   What does Kye think? _____

   _____

   What does Victor think? _____

   _____

3. Jody and Dee babysit for the same family. Lately Jody gets all the jobs from this family.

   What does Jody think? _____

   _____

   What does Dee think? _____

   _____

# Point of View

Read each situation.  Then write what each character probably thinks about the situation.

1. Omar and Dale agreed to take care of a neighbor's cat while the neighbors were on vacation.  When Omar called Dale to plan when they would take care of the cat, Dale said he didn't like cats and didn't want to be around the neighbor's cat.

   What does Omar think? _____

   _____

   What does Dale think? _____

   _____

2. Mia studied hard for a math test today.  Kevin didn't study much.  The teacher just postponed the test for a week.

   What does Mia think? _____

   _____

   What does Kevin think? _____

   _____

3. Parker and Mike saw someone shoplift in a convenience store.  Parker wants to report the person to a cashier but Mike doesn't.

   What does Parker think? _____

   _____

   What does Mike think? _____

   _____

3. Ron and Erick both like the same girl.  She used to pay attention to both of them, but lately, she only pays attention to Erick.

   What does Ron think? _____

   _____

   What does Erick think? _____

   _____

# Empathizing ❶

Read each situation.  Then check the comment that shows the most empathy for the person in the situation.

1. Sherise's parents are getting a divorce.  She is upset and doesn't want the divorce to change her relationship with either of her parents.
   - ☐ a. "Which parent are you going to live with?"
   - ☐ b. "It's tough when your parents just can't get along."
   - ☐ c. "You should stay with your dad.  He's really cool."

2. Derek is the starting pitcher for the school team.  Yesterday at practice, he sprained his wrist.  His doctor said he shouldn't pitch for four weeks.  Derek will have to miss four very important games of the season.
   - ☐ a. "That's a rough break, Derek.  You must be disappointed."
   - ☐ b. "Just forget about it.  There's nothing you can do to change it."
   - ☐ c. "Look on the bright side.  You get a break from pitching!"

3. John's older brother, Troy, signed up for the Marines.  Now that Troy has graduated from high school, he will leave for boot camp in one week.  John is proud of Troy for serving the country, but he'll really miss Troy.
   - ☐ a. "I bet you're glad Troy won't be around to tell you what to do now."
   - ☐ b. "That's what happens when people grow up; they leave home."
   - ☐ c. "It must be hard to see Troy go, even though you're proud of him."

4. Kelly and her best friend, Danielle, tried out for the cheerleading squad.  Kelly made the squad but Danielle didn't.  Kelly is thrilled for herself but sorry Danielle didn't make it.
   - ☐ a. "It must be awkward for you with Danielle, but I know you'll make sure you stay her best friend."
   - ☐ b. "Danielle just isn't as good at cheerleading as you are."
   - ☐ c. "Danielle can try again next year.  Don't worry about her."

5. Riley spends lots of time studying, but he doesn't get good grades.  He just got his report card and he's disappointed with his low grades.
   - ☐ a. "That's okay, no one cares what grades you get."
   - ☐ b. "You try hard but it doesn't seem to help.  That must be frustrating."
   - ☐ c. "Why don't you try using a tutor or getting some help?"

6. Deanne's little sister keeps using Deanne's makeup and borrowing her clothes, no matter how many times Deanne asks her not to.
   - ☐ a. "You should make your mom punish her."
   - ☐ b. "It's so annoying having a little sister use your stuff without your permission!"
   - ☐ c. "Borrow some of her things.  That will teach her not to take yours."

# Empathizing ❷

Read each situation. Then check the comment that shows the most empathy for the person in the situation.

1. Cole's mother has just been diagnosed with breast cancer. Her doctors are hopeful she will overcome the cancer with treatment, but it will take a long time.
   - ☐ a. "What will the doctors do for your mom?"
   - ☐ b. "I'll bet you're worried. That's a real shock to you and your family."
   - ☐ c. "Your mom looks great. I'm sure she'll be just fine."

2. Brian spent all weekend working on his report. He couldn't finish it and it's due today.
   - ☐ a. "It's just a book report. Just turn it in late."
   - ☐ b. "Why didn't you finish your report? You worked on it all weekend."
   - ☐ c. "It's frustrating when you worked so hard but you still couldn't finish."

3. Mike and Rory have been best friends for years. Rory's family is moving to another state and Mike won't see him for a long time.
   - ☐ a. "It's easy to stay in touch with e-mail and text messaging."
   - ☐ b. "You probably wonder what you'll do without Rory. He's your best friend."
   - ☐ c. "Maybe you could have a going-away party for Rory."

4. Lucy did fine in her drivers' ed class, but today she failed the driving test at the license bureau.
   - ☐ a. "You should have practiced driving more before you took the test."
   - ☐ b. "You don't really need to drive a car yet anyway."
   - ☐ c. "That's embarrassing, but at least you know you did well in the class."

5. Sarah wants Ned to ask her to the dance, but Ned asked someone else.
   - ☐ a. "Ouch! I know you were hoping he would ask you to this dance."
   - ☐ b. "There are plenty of other guys who might ask you to the dance."
   - ☐ c. "Maybe you should dress better so Ned would notice you more."

6. Latrice's mom often loses her temper. She yells at Latrice even when something isn't Latrice's fault.
   - ☐ a. "You should just yell back at your mom."
   - ☐ b. "Don't worry if your mom yells at you. Just don't listen to her."
   - ☐ c. "It's tough when she yells at you, especially when you don't deserve it."

7. Brenda's grandpa died last week and they were very close.
   - ☐ a. "How old was your grandpa?"
   - ☐ b. "I'm sorry about your grandpa. You must miss him already."
   - ☐ c. "At least it wasn't your dad who died."

# Empathizing ❸

Read each situation. Then check the comment that shows the most empathy for the person in the situation.

1. Derek just got his math test back and it's another *D*. He's worried he won't pass this course and it will look bad on his record.
   - ☐ a. "Why didn't you study better for the test?"
   - ☐ b. "You must be wondering if you can pass this course."
   - ☐ c. "Nobody cares what grades you got once you graduate."

2. Chantel's mom just got married again. This will be her second stepdad. Chantel doesn't know her new stepdad very well yet.
   - ☐ a. "It must be awkward to have a stepdad you hardly know."
   - ☐ b. "Just stay away from your new stepdad for a while."
   - ☐ c. "My stepdad is really great."

3. While Chip was grounded, his neighbor saw him sneak out a window and told Chip's dad. Chip thinks now he'll be grounded for twice as long.
   - ☐ a. "You should tell your neighbor to just mind her own business."
   - ☐ b. "You are anxious about what your parents will do."
   - ☐ c. "You knew you were taking a risk."

4. Ramon worked hard on his science project, but compared to everyone else's, his looked messy and he's embarrassed.
   - ☐ a. "I'm glad my project looks okay."
   - ☐ b. "Yours isn't horrible, it's just a little sloppy."
   - ☐ c. "I can tell your project took a lot of work and what you found out is more important than how your display looks."

5. When Tina watches TV, her mom always lets her little sister choose the show.
   - ☐ a. "It must be annoying to have to give in to your little sister."
   - ☐ b. "There are plenty of other things to do besides watch TV."
   - ☐ c. "Maybe you should tell your mom she isn't being fair to you."

6. Drew's family is moving away and he knows he'll miss his friends a lot.
   - ☐ a. "You should just make some new friends as fast as you can."
   - ☐ b. "It's a bummer that you have to move and we'll miss you."
   - ☐ c. "I moved two years ago and it was easy to meet everyone here."

7. Brett got a note asking him to come to the principal's office, but he doesn't know why.
   - ☐ a. "What did you do wrong?"
   - ☐ b. "Maybe he sent the note to the wrong person."
   - ☐ c. "You're anxious about why the principal wants to see you."

# Stating a Problem ❶

Practice stating a problem clearly.

Photo courtesy of istockphoto.com © Eileen Hart

1. Nicole shares a room with her sister, Denise. They get along well but they have different ideas about the way they keep their room clean. Nicole puts her dirty clothes in the laundry and always makes her bed. Denise leaves her clothes lying on her bed or the floor. Nicole usually ignores her sister's mess, but today a friend is coming over to visit and will be in the girls' bedroom.

    Pretend you are Nicole. Write your problem.

    _____

    _____

    Pretend you are Denise. Write your problem. _____

    _____

2. Cassie is spending the night at Lori's home. Cassie is a vegetarian. Lori doesn't know Cassie's a vegetarian and made a special spaghetti meat sauce for dinner.

    Pretend you are Cassie. Write your problem. _____

    _____

    Pretend you are Lori. Write your problem. _____

    _____

3. Jeffrey and Damion want to use the computer to do homework. Jeffrey's report is due tomorrow. Damion's poem is due in two days.

    Pretend you are Jeffrey. Write your problem. _____

    _____

    Pretend you are Damion. Write your problem. _____

    _____

# Stating a Problem ❷

Practice stating a problem clearly.

1. Gloria takes school seriously and wants to go to college. Ray also wants to go to college, but he doesn't study and most of his classes don't interest him. Today Ray is trying to copy Gloria's answers on a test. Gloria is trying to shield her paper.

   Pretend you are Gloria. Write your problem. _____

   _____

   Pretend you are Ray. Write your problem. _____

   _____

2. Vinny has a part-time job. His boss wants him to work an extra two hours today to help with a special project. Vinny has homework and his dad won't allow him to stay up after 10:00 p.m.

   Pretend you are Vinny. Write your problem. _____

   _____

3. LuAnn usually babysits Saturday evenings for Mrs. Parsons, but this Saturday, LuAnn wants to go to the movies with some friends. Mrs. Parsons doesn't trust anyone else to babysit her children.

   Pretend you are LuAnn. Write your problem. _____

   _____

4. Nick and Kurt enjoy riding their bikes. They are planning a long ride for this coming Saturday. Nick wants a ride with lots of hills. Kurt wants a smooth ride with as few hills as possible.

   Pretend you are Nick. Write your problem. _____

   _____

   Pretend you are Kurt. Write your problem. _____

   _____

# Stating a Problem ❸

Practice stating a problem clearly.

1. Liz and Dan are deciding where to sit in the theater to see the new movie *Beware!* Liz doesn't like loud noises and wants to sit toward the back. Dan wants to sit toward the front so he can feel closer to the action in the movie.

   Pretend you are Liz. Write your problem. _____

   _____

   Pretend you are Dan. Write your problem. _____

   _____

2. Julio tries to follow rules and avoid getting into trouble. His good friend Miguel likes to take risks and often breaks rules. Miguel wants Julio to go through some new homes under construction while no workers are around. Julio doesn't want to go with Miguel.

   Pretend you are Julio. Write your problem. _____

   _____

   Pretend you are Miguel. Write your problem. _____

   _____

3. Tricia and Elaine are supposed to visit their grandmother in a nursing home today. They can walk to the home from where they live. Tricia wants to spend two hours with her grandmother because she enjoys talking with her. Elaine has to practice piano and has about three hours of homework tonight, so she wants to spend only one hour with her grandmother.

   Pretend you are Tricia. Write your problem. _____

   _____

   Pretend you are Elaine. Write your problem. _____

   _____

# Talking It Over

When you disagree with a friend, it helps to talk it over. Think about how the conversation will go ahead of time. Use these "talking heads" to imagine what you will say and your friend will say. Point to "Me" and tell your friend how you feel and why. Then pretend to be "My Friend" and say what your friend would say. Try to keep the conversation going, playing both roles, until you think you and your friend understand the situation and how you both feel about it.

**Me**                     **My Friend**

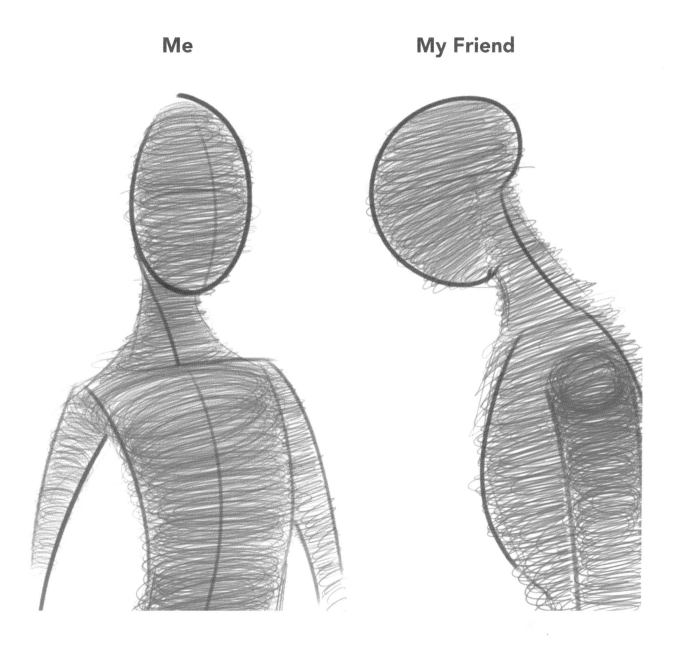

# Stating Solutions ❶

When two people disagree, it helps for both people to think of possible solutions.  Think of as many solutions as you can for each disagreement.  State each solution clearly.

1.  Melissa and Marcy want to study together for a math test.  Melissa thinks they should make up practice problems to solve.  Marcy wants to review the textbook chapter and her notes from class.

    _____

    _____

    _____

2.  Patrice and Christy are shopping for a birthday present for their mom.  Patrice wants to buy her a new purse.  Christy wants to make coupons for doing extra chores that would help their mom.

    _____

    _____

    _____

3.  Diego shares a room with his older brother, Ricardo.  Diego takes good care of his things and doesn't like Ricardo to borrow or use anything without his permission.  Ricardo thinks Diego is too uptight about his things and, as his older brother, he should be able to use Diego's things without getting his permission.

    _____

    _____

    _____

4.  Wanda and Tom both prefer to watch the biggest TV at home, but they disagree about which shows to watch.

    _____

    _____

    _____

# Stating Solutions ❷

Think of as many solutions as you can for each disagreement. State each solution clearly.

1. JoEllen and Tom have been dating for a long time. This Saturday JoEllen wants to go see a new romance movie but Tom doesn't want to see that movie.

   _____

   _____

   _____

2. Mrs. Jenkins stayed at home while her children were young, but now she will start a full-time job. Her daughters disagree about who should do which chores to help out. Neither of them wants to be responsible for cleaning the bathrooms or doing the laundry. Mrs. Jenkins wants the girls to settle their disagreement on their own.

   _____

   _____

   _____

3. Troy and Tina won the first place trophy for their bulletin board display about world hunger. They each want to keep the trophy.

   _____

   _____

   _____

4. Construction has blocked the way Jerry and Dan usually ride their bikes to school. Jerry thinks they should still ride their bikes and take the four-block detour. Dan thinks they should walk instead because the detour would take them through main streets with heavy traffic.

   _____

   _____

   _____

# One-Sided vs. Mutual Solutions

When the solution to a disagreement only pleases one person, it is a one-sided solution. A solution that pleases both people is a mutual solution.

Write **OS** in the blank if a solution is one-sided. Write **M** if a solution is mutual.

1. Reggie and Victor are choosing a restaurant for the family's supper. Reggie wants to eat Italian food. Victor wants Southern-fried chicken.

   _____ Solution: The family will go to Grandma's Chicken Palace.

2. Tina and Sue both want an apple, but there is only one left.

   _____ Solution: They will split the apple.

3. Roger needs to take out the trash and Brandon wants to shoot hoops with Roger.

   _____ Solution: After Roger takes out the trash, the boys will shoot hoops.

4. Pat and Erin are sisters. They both like a sweater at a garage sale, but there is only one.

   _____ Solution: They will buy the sweater and take turns wearing it.

5. Hank and Dave both need the resource book for a school project. They can't check it out of the library.

   _____ Solution: Hank will let Dave use the book.

6. Carrie and Nancy are going to the movies. Carrie wants to invite Danica to join them but Nancy doesn't want Danica along.

   _____ Solution: They don't invite Danica to join them.

7. Roy and Dino both want to play the piano. There is only one piano.

   _____ Solution: The boys will take 15-minute turns playing the piano.

8. Gregg and Dale are hiking. They come to a crossing trail. Gregg wants to take a turn to the left. Dale wants to take a turn to the right.

   _____ Solution: They agree to keep going straight ahead.

9. Yvonne and Darla agreed to meet for lunch on Saturday. Yvonne wants to meet at 11:30. Darla wants to meet at 1:00.

   _____ Solution: They will meet at 11:30.

# One-Sided vs. Mutual Solutions

When the solution to a disagreement only pleases one person, it is a one-sided solution. A solution that pleases both people is a mutual solution.

Write **OS** in the blank if a solution is one-sided.  Write **M** if a solution is mutual.

1. Josie and Phil are relaxing in their family room.  Josie wants Phil to turn the volume down on the music he's playing.  Phil likes the volume the way it is.

   _____ Solution:  Josie will wear ear plugs or go to another room.

2. Maya and Lee enjoy making jewelry with beads.  Together they designed and made a necklace and a set of matching earrings.  They each want to keep the special jewelry.

   _____ Solution:  Maya will keep the earrings and Lee will keep the necklace.

3. Pete and Marvin both want to ask Sandra to the dance next week.

   _____ Solution:  Pete will ask Sandra first.

4. Claire and Sonia are at the beach.  Claire has had enough sun and wants to be in the shade.  Sonia wants to get more sun.

   _____ Solution:  They will move to a spot on the beach that has both shade and sun.

5. Carol and Lois are ordering a birthday cake for a party.  Carol wants it to be chocolate.  Lois wants a vanilla cake.

   _____ Solution:  They will order a vanilla cake with chocolate frosting.

6. Gail and Deb share a bedroom.  Gail likes fresh air and wants to open the window.  Deb has allergies and wants the window to stay closed.

   _____ Solution:  The window will stay closed.

7. Otis and Gary both want to be scorekeepers for bowling.

   _____ Solution:  They will take turns.  Each one will be scorekeeper for a game.

8. The Bensons will order a large pizza for dinner.  Jill wants pepperoni.  Dawn wants mushrooms and no meat.

   _____ Solution:  The Bensons will order a half-and-half pizza.

9. Lori and Anna both want to keep a pretty mirror they found in a parking lot.

   _____ Solution:  Anna will keep the mirror.

# Reaching a Compromise ❶

Sometimes a compromise is the best way to settle a disagreement. Both partners talk together and each give up something to make a deal that satisfies both of them. Here's an example:

Naomi wears trendy clothes and is proud of the tattoos on her arms. Her mom is embarrassed about the way Naomi looks, especially in front of Grandma. Grandma is coming to visit next weekend. Naomi's mom asks her to dress more traditionally and to cover her tattoos while Grandma is there. Naomi thinks it shouldn't make any difference what she wears, especially at home.

Here is one way they could compromise to settle this disagreement:

• Naomi can wear whatever she likes, as long as she keeps her tattoos covered.

For each disagreement, think of a way the partners could reach a compromise.

1. Chad and his dad eat dinner together once a week at a restaurant. Tonight Chad wants a hamburger and his dad wants Chinese food. How could they compromise?

   _____

2. Rick and Bryce both want to use the family computer for an hour tonight for their homework. They both want to work right after supper. How could they compromise?

   _____

3. Louisa and Moe share a bedroom and they have different ideas about how their room should be kept. Louisa wants everything put away neatly all the time. Moe wants to put things away and tidy up the room just once a week. How could they compromise?

   _____

4. B.J. and Mark are brothers. B.J. is in a small band that practices in his home. Mark can't concentrate to do his homework when the band is practicing. How could these brothers compromise?

   _____

# Reaching a Compromise ❷

For each disagreement, think of a way the partners could reach a compromise.

1. Sherrie and her mom are trying to decide where to go for their vacation. Sherrie wants to go to a beach and swim. Her mom wants to be somewhere surrounded by mountains. How could they compromise?

   _____

2. Friends Todd and Jesse bought a remote control airplane together. They each paid half of the money. They each want to store the plane at home. How could they compromise?

   _____

3. Carissa and Ming want to see a movie on Saturday. Carissa wants to go to the earliest showing. Ming wants to go the 9:00 p.m. showing. How could they compromise?

   _____

4. Mike and Aaron have to share a bathroom. They get up at the same time and want to use the bathroom to shower and get ready for school. How could they compromise?

   _____

5. Tracy wants to be with her friends every night, but her twin wants her to stay home with her. How could they compromise?

   _____

6. Jose and Calvin are starting a games club at school. Jose wants it to focus on computer games but Calvin wants to include card games and board games. How could they compromise?

   _____

7. Moira and Leah are in charge of a fashion show. They each want to be the narrator for the show. How could they compromise?

   _____

8. Doreen and Trish agreed to paint a mural at school. Doreen wants to show children from different cultures dancing. Trish wants to show the new fountain in the center of town. How could they compromise?

   _____

# Giving Reasons for Solutions

When you state a way to settle a disagreement, tell the reason it would be a good solution so people know what you're thinking.

Think of a good solution for each disagreement.  Tell why it would be a good solution.

1. Lester and Cody want to practice shooting baskets.  They only have one basketball.

   Solution: _____

   Reason: _____

2. Jared and Sheryl have to share a car.  Jared wants the car tonight to take a friend to a movie.  Sheryl wants the car tonight to go out to dinner with her friends.

   Solution: _____

   Reason: _____

3. Marty's mom wants her to babysit her younger brother on Saturday from noon until 6:00 p.m.  Marty wants to meet her friends at 4:00 Saturday afternoon.

   Solution: _____

   Reason: _____

4. David and Glen signed up to play a duet in the variety show.  David wants to practice four times a week until the show, but Glen wants to practice just once a week.

   Solution: _____

   Reason: _____

5. Daryl is visiting Bryce.  While making themselves lunch, they made a mess of the kitchen.  Bryce wants Daryl to help clean up the mess, but Daryl would rather play a game on Bryce's computer instead.

   Solution: _____

   Reason: _____

6. Gayle and Deedee found a $50 bill on the sidewalk and each want to keep it.

   Solution: _____

   Reason: _____

# Maintaining a Relationship

When you disagree with someone, decide which is more important – winning the argument or maintaining the relationship with the person. Good friends value their friendship more than winning an argument.

Check each way to settle a disagreement that would maintain a good relationship with a friend.

☐ 1. Tell your friend that your solution is the only one that makes sense.

☐ 2. Talk with your friend about ways you could each compromise.

☐ 3. Show that you are stronger than your friend.

☐ 4. Ask someone else to tell you both what to do.

☐ 5. Agree to ignore the disagreement.

☐ 6. Tell your friend why you deserve to win the argument.

☐ 7. Threaten not to talk to your friend anymore.

☐ 8. Make fun of your friend.

☐ 9. Agree to whatever your friend wants.

☐ 10. Tell your friend that you will do what he wants this time, but next time, you hope your friend will agree to do what you want.

☐ 11. Tell your friend your friendship is more important to you than whatever you are arguing about.

☐ 12. Avoid talking to your friend until you get your way.

☐ 13. Remind your friend that you usually know best.

☐ 14. Ask your friend what would make your friendship even stronger.

☐ 15. Ask your friend if it's okay to toss a coin to decide which one of you will win the argument.

# "Fair" Isn't Always Equal

When you disagree with someone, think about fairness when you try to settle the disagreement. Being fair doesn't always mean treating people equally. Being fair means giving people what they need. To think of a fair solution, ask yourself, "What does this person need?"

Read each situation and follow the directions.

1. You and a friend walked to the mall a few hours ago. Your friend's legs are tired from shopping. She wants to take a bus home, but she's not allowed to ride a public bus alone. You don't want to spend the money for a bus ride and your legs feel fine.

   Think of a fair solution to this problem. Tell why it would be fair.

   _____

   _____

2. You and a friend are doing homework in the same room. You usually play music in the background while you do your work, so you turn on some music. Your friend has a learning disability that makes it tough for him to concentrate on his work unless it's quiet.

   Think of a good solution to this problem. Tell why it would be fair.

   _____

   _____

3. You and a friend agree to go to a movie. Your friend wants to see a movie rated PG-13 but you are only allowed to see G-rated movies.

   Think of a good solution to this problem. Tell why it would be fair.

   _____

   _____

# Role-Playing Situations ❶

Take turns playing the role of each character in these situations. First find a partner. Then talk with your partner to decide who will play the role of each character. The goal of each role-play is to reach an agreement that satisfies both you and your partner.

Keep these tips in mind as you negotiate with your partner:

- Try to understand what your partner thinks and feels about the situation. Watch for nonverbal clues that signal how your partner feels.

- State your suggestions and opinions about what to do clearly. Tell why your suggestions or opinions make good sense for both of you.

- Think of a compromise or a way to settle things so that both of you are happy.

- Consider your partner a friend. Which is more important to you, winning in this situation or keeping your friendship strong?

1. **Person A:** You and your partner agreed to play a game. You want to play Monopoly.

    **Person B:** You want to play UNO because you don't like a game that takes a long time to play.

2. **Person A:** You want your friend to earn money by offering to shovel snow off your neighbors' driveways and sidewalks.

    **Person B:** You like the idea of working with your friend to earn money, but you don't want to shovel snow.

3. **Person A:** You usually walk to school with your friend. Lately some bullies have been bothering you on one block. You want to take a different route to school. The new route would be four blocks longer.

    **Person B:** You like to walk to school with your friend and you're not scared of the bullies as long as you are with your friend. You don't want to take extra time to walk a longer way to school.

4. **Person A:** You are planning a party with your friend. You want to invite a new student your friends don't know very well yet.

    **Person B:** You want the party to be with just your good friends. You don't want to invite the new student.

5. **Person A:** You and your friend are in the same biology class. You will have a mid-term test in one week. You want to study with your friend because it helps you to talk about what you have learned and what might be on the test.

    **Person B:** You would much rather study by yourself. It's easier for you to remember what you learn if you reread your notes and your textbook.

# Role-Playing Situations ❷

Take turns playing the role of each character in these situations. First find a partner. Then talk with your partner to decide who will play the role of each character. The goal of each role-play is to reach an agreement that satisfies both you and your partner.

1.  Person A:  You and your friend want to plan a going-away event for another friend who is moving. You want to get all your friends together and go bowling because the friend moving away likes to bowl.

    Person B:  You don't like to bowl and you know some of the friends you would invite don't like to bowl either. You would rather have everyone meet at a nearby park to play basketball and have snacks.

2.  Person A:  You and Person B agreed to perform a guitar duet in the school variety show. You want to practice together every day until the show, which is two weeks away.

    Person B:  You have after-school activities scheduled three days a week. You don't want to miss these activities and you think the two of you already know your duet well enough that you don't have to practice every day.

3.  Person A:  You agreed to go to your favorite pizza place with Person B. Then your mom said you must take your younger brother with you if you go. You promised your mom you would take him with you.

    Person B:  You don't want to have Person A's younger brother go with you to the pizza place.

4.  Person A:  You want Person B to go to a party at a friend's apartment. The friend lives on the second floor and there is no elevator.

    Person B:  You need to use a wheelchair. You would be embarrassed if your friends had to carry you up to the second floor.

5.  Person A:  Your parents grounded you for misbehaving. You are allowed to visit Person B to do homework together, but you are not allowed to hang out with your other friends for two weeks. You decide to be with your friends anyway and you want Person B to cover for you by saying you are doing homework together.

    Person B:  You understand why Person A wants to ignore being grounded, but you don't want to lie about it.

6.  Person A:  You and your friend need to write a report about a museum visit for English. You want to go to an art museum and see the paintings and sculptures.

    Person B:  You would rather go to a museum with interactive exhibits, like the Museum of Science and Industry.

7.  Person A:  You and your friend are at an amusement park. You want to ride the giant roller coaster and some of the other wild rides.

    Person B:  Wild rides make you sick to your stomach. You would rather ride bumper cars or throw things to earn prizes.

# Role-Playing Situations ❸

Take turns playing the role of each character in these situations. First find a partner. Then talk with your partner to decide who will play the role of each character. The goal of each role-play is to reach an agreement that satisfies both you and your partner.

1. **Person A:** You are planning a hike with Person B. You have one trail guide to help you plan your hike. You both want to use the trail guide to plan your hike over the weekend. You live several miles from Person B and neither of you can drive a car.
   **Person B:** You want to use the trail guide over the weekend.

2. **Person A:** Your principal has asked volunteers to help clean up the litter around the school grounds this afternoon after school. You want to walk home with Person B as you normally do, but you'd like to spend half an hour helping with the cleanup before you go home.
   **Person B:** You have a lot of homework and you are eager to get home as soon as possible so you can get started on your assignments.

3. **Person A:** You and Person B both want to ask the same person to the school dance. Neither of you has ever asked Person C out before.
   **Person B:** You want to ask the same person to the school dance.

4. **Person A:** You and Person B agreed to go somewhere Saturday. You want to leave home before noon, but you have several chores to do at home before you can leave. You want Person B to spend the night Friday and help you do your chores Saturday morning so you can both leave before noon.
   **Person B:** You already have plans for Friday night and you don't want to help with Person A's chores before you leave on Saturday.

5. **Person A:** You and Person B want to join a school club together. You want to join the debate club because you enjoy giving speeches and sharing your opinions. You like to interact with other students, so you are eager to talk with and listen to other students in whatever club you join.
   **Person B:** You want to join the chess club. You hate speaking in front of a group, and you don't enjoy making small talk.

6. **Person A:** You and Person B are reading books together. You like to hear music while you read.
   **Person B:** When you read, you don't want to hear music or anything else that distracts you. You prefer to read in quiet surroundings.

7. **Person A:** You and Person B are supposed to paint a mural for a bulletin board in the hall. You want to use bright colors and make an abstract design.
   **Person B:** You want to make a political statement with your mural about the reasons we should take care of the environment.

# Answer Key

The answers given are examples of expected responses. Accept other logical answers as correct.

**Page 6**
1. any problem reasonably resolved via negotiation between the parties
2. pleases both parties
3. Watching TV is boring; I want to do something more energetic.
4. We can wait to decide what to do.
5. She wants to leave now but her friend doesn't.
6. She wants to stay but her friend wants to leave.
7. compromise re: how long to stay, leave now because of Nora's need
8. take turns
9. flip a coin
10. talk about doing something else together

**Page 7**
Checked boxes: 1, 3, 4, 7, 9, 10

**Page 9**
1. alternatives
2. motivate
3. long-term
4. conflict
5. inference
6. empathy
7. interpersonal
8. paraphrase
9. perspective
10. yield
11. drawback
12. mutual

**Page 10**
1. consequence
2. negotiation
3. personal
4. dominate
5. short-term
6. solution
7. benefit
8. ineffective
9. one-sided
10. compromise
11. flexible
12. strategy

**Page 11**
Checked boxes: 1, 3, 4, 6
7. female
8. adolescent
9. car
10. car keys

11. happy, pleased
12. got new car/license

**Pages 12-14**
Answers will vary.

**Page 15**
1. I wish I would get to school on time.
2. Who is Olivia dating?
3. I don't like comedies nearly as well as action movies.
4. My pitching was bad all through the game.
5. I need it quiet so I can think.
6. Sonia ignores me.
7. I'd rather play the guitar than play basketball.
8. I can't tell what Byron thinks because he doesn't talk much.
9. Just ask me if you want advice.

**Page 16**
1. Geometry is hard for me.
2. Allison doesn't pay attention to me.
3. I wish I had no homework for a week.
4. We should get there early while the line is still short.
5. You should walk in that park before sunset.
6. I wish Tory would ask me.
7. Breaking his glasses was an accident.
8. We could leave unnoticed now.
9. Don't bother me.
10. Tracy is half an hour late.
11. I don't like people to gossip about me.

**Pages 17-18**
Answers will vary.

**Page 19**
1. Hao: We can race through this stuff because it's simple.
   Lian: I wish he would slow down. It's hard for me to understand.
2. Kye: I want to go after 11 a.m. and stay all day.
   Victor: I want to go early to be home by 2 p.m.

3. Jody: I'm lucky to get more jobs.
   Dee: Why does Jody get more jobs? I'm jealous.

**Page 20**
1. Omar: Dale should keep his promise.
   Dale: I shouldn't have agreed to do it.
2. Mia: I'm disappointed.
   Kevin: Great news!
3. Parker: It's the right thing to do.
   Mike: It's not our business.
4. Ron: I'm disappointed/hurt.
   Erick: Lucky me!

**Page 21**
1. B    4. A
2. A    5. B
3. C    6. B

**Page 22**
1. B    5. A
2. C    6. C
3. B    7. B
4. C

**Page 23**
1. B    5. A
2. A    6. B
3. B    7. C
4. C

**Page 24**
1. Nicole: I don't want my friend to see our bedroom a mess.
   Denise: It's not my problem if Nicole is embarrassed.
2. Cassie: I don't eat meat but I don't want to hurt my friend's feelings.
   Lori: I want Cassie to enjoy the special meal I fixed.
3. Jeffrey: I need the computer because my assignment is due before Damion's.
   Damion: I need the computer so I can make changes easily to my poem.

**Page 25**
1. Gloria: I don't want him to cheat from my paper.
   Ray: I need to get a good grade.
2. I can't please my boss and do my homework before 10:00.
3. I am trapped by my babysitting job.
4. Nick: I want to challenge my body by riding the hills.
   Kurt: I want to enjoy the ride, not work hard on hills.

**Page 26**
1. Liz: I won't enjoy the movie if we sit close to the screen.
   Dan: The movie won't be as exciting if we sit far back.
2. Julio: I don't want to get into trouble.
   Miguel: I want my friend along with me.
3. Tricia: I don't want a short visit with Grandma.
   Elaine: I don't have time to spend hours with Grandma today.

**Page 28-29**
Answers will vary.

**Page 30**
1. OS    6. OS
2. M     7. M
3. M     8. M
4. M     9. OS
5. OS

**Page 31**
1. OS    6. OS
2. M     7. M
3. OS    8. M
4. M     9. OS
5. M

**Pages 32-34**
Answers will vary.

**Page 35**
Checked boxes: 2, 5, 9, 10, 11, 14, 15

**Pages 36-39**
Answers will vary.